RESTAURANT 2000

dining design III

RESTAURANT 2000

dining design III

Christy Casamassima

foreword by Adam D. Tihany

PBC INTERNATIONAL, INC.

Distributor to the book trade in the United States and Canada
Rizzoli International Publications, Inc.
through St. Martin's Press
175 Fifth Avenue
New York, NY 10010

Distributor to the art trade in the United States and Canada
PBC International, Inc.
One School Street
Glen Cove, NY 11542

Distributor throughout the rest of the world
Hearst Books International
1350 Avenue of the Americas
New York, NY 10019

Library of Congress Cataloging-in-Publication Data
Casamassima, Christy.
    Restaurant 2000 : dining design III / by Christy Casamassima.
      p.   cm.
  Includes index.
  ISBN 0-86636-586-9 (hardbound). — ISBN 0-86636-587-7 (pbk.)
  1. Restaurants—Decoration—United States. I. Title
NK2195.R4C37 1998
725'.71—dc21   98-22351
                               CIP

CAVEAT—Information in this text is believed accurate, and will pose no
problem for the student or casual reader. However, the author was often
constrained by information contained in signed release forms, information
that could have been in error or not included at all. Any misinformation
(or lack of information) is the result of failure in these attestations. The
author has done whatever is possible to insure accuracy.

10 9 8 7 6 5 4 3 2 1

Printed in Hong Kong

To my father,
Matthew Casamassima,
whose passion for good food
and enthusiasm for all things culinary,
continues to enrich many lives.

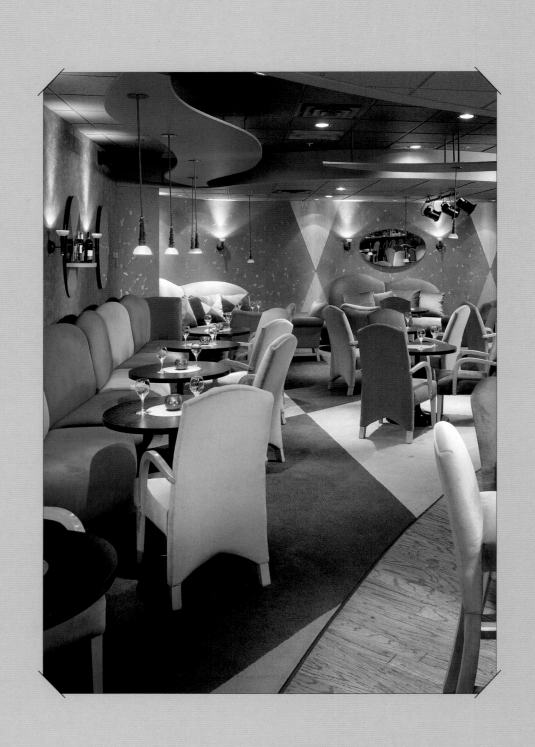

specialties

FOREWORD

As the millennium approaches and our global community expands, restaurants all over the world are blending, sharing and offering a more unified "universal language" of food. It is for this reason that design has become a major element of any restaurant's business, on a par with cuisine and service, in drawing and keeping the customer. In this era when chefs are celebrities, restaurants are theatres and the public knows all and bares all, restaurateurs and restaurant designers must deliver highly detailed, beautiful and imaginative restaurants. Image and fantasy are necessities, but true substance is what will set a restaurant apart from its competition.

Graziella Vigo

A great restaurant design has long surpassed the mere search for a new style or the interpretation of a visual concept. It has become an in-depth study of demographics, social conditions, an integration of moods and signals, and finally, a scientific knowledge of space and planning. The responsibility of the designer does not stop at creating an appealing visual magnet; it also must extend to creating environments conducive for operators to perform well enough so their customers will return again and again.

One of the most important aspects of creating a successful restaurant is consistency. From the front doorknob, through each and every design element of the architecture and furnishings, it is the designer's responsibility to deliver a sensory experience compatible with the level of service and the taste of food that the client anticipates. Only when these ingredients are tightly knit and complementary will the restaurant achieve that seamless, elusive consistency and become a complete experience that will remain embedded in the customer's memory. It is this harmony of elements, this tapestry of the senses, that creates restaurants capable of leading us into the year 2000.

ADAM D. TIHANY

INTRODUCTION

Diners are increasingly demanding when it comes to selecting a restaurant. Innovative cuisine, once the star of the show, is no longer sufficient to draw and sustain patrons, particularly in urban areas like New York City which boasts one of the most varied and competitive restaurant scenes in the world.

Amanda Fairchild

Internationally, diners with an appetite for entertainment—as well as fine food—crave a setting that provides ambience, comfort, and diversion from the working world. Designers have responded to the call by creating distinctive environments with unique personalities. Each venue featured in *Restaurant 2000; Dining Design III* stimulates the senses through a fusion of customized raw materials, creative lighting, and bold decor—elements that enhance each culinary concept and create a memorable dining experience.

One of the most pervasive trends in contemporary restaurant design is to place patrons in the center of the action by literally knocking down walls and eliminating visual barriers between a venue's kitchen, bar, and dining areas. To the delight of diners and proud chefs, these open layouts with exposed kitchens, glass wine cellars, and enticing food displays provide a sumptuous feast for the eyes as well as the taste buds.

In the past decade, restaurant design has reached new heights, blending elements of modern architecture, lighting, and decor to create functional showplaces like those within the pages of *Restaurant 2000; Dining Design III*. With so much attention and capital riding on a venue's success, restaurateurs are turning to designers with celebrity status to add cutting-edge cachet to projects, elevating restaurant design to an art form, and catapulting dining out into the next millennium.

CHRISTY CASAMASSIMA

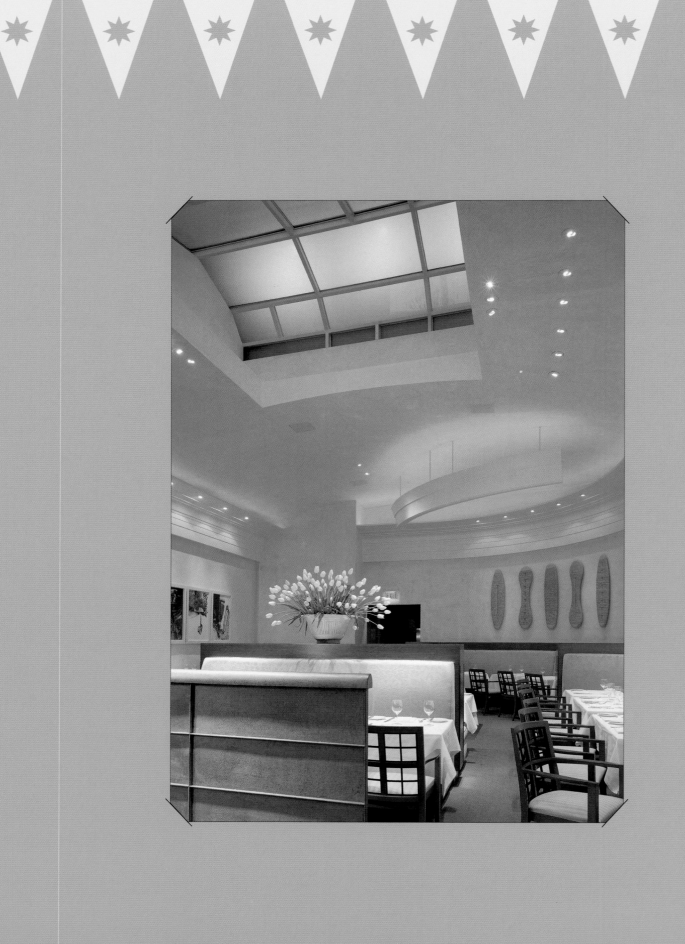

timeless

Opus 251

Cub Room

Pinot Bistro

Vertigo Restaurant & Bar

Water Grill

Provence Restaurant

Cafe Spiaggia

Angelo & Maxie's Steakhouse

On Canon

Tammany Hall

Luma

Jean Georges Restaurant

OPUS 251

PHILADELPHIA, PENNSYLVANIA

Set in The Art Alliance Building, a landmark museum on historic Rittenhouse Square, Opus 251 was designed with maximum respect for the features of the original arts annex. Today, although the restaurant retains refined and elegant details of the former museum, its style is decidedly casual and rustic—like that of a private home. In an eight-week renovation, the designers and the owner set out to create a warm and intimate dining spot. The soft color in the main dining room was chosen to take a back seat to the 80-year-old Asian mural that

frames the upper portion of the dining area. The subtle background contrasts with the bold red that saturates walls in the bar area, where windows offer an expansive view. Handcrafted period moldings, fireplaces, arches, paneled walls, chandeliers, and sculptures create an ambience that transports patrons back to an era when arts and culture were integrated into everyday life. From the dining room, French doors open onto a charming outdoor garden, which also can be viewed from the handsome bar area.

timeless

previous page The designers chose subdued wall colors to offset the beautiful
Asian mural that decorates the dining room. left A mirrored display area gives
the illusion of an expanded space without altering the original structure.
above An antique chandelier casts a warm glow on the bar area, which
overlooks the garden. next spread Wide plank floors, wood paneled walls,
dramatic archways, and original artifacts evoke a sense of history and culture.

ARCHITECT/INTERIOR DESIGNER: *Floss Barber, Inc.*
SQUARE FEET/METERS: *1,300 / 121*
DESIGN BUDGET: *$170,000*
SEATING: *84*
CHECK AVERAGE: *$50*
PHOTOGRAPHER: *© Matt Wargo*

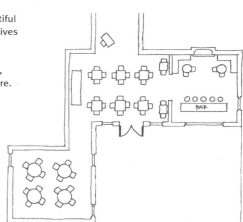

CUB ROOM

NEW YORK, NEW YORK

Henry Meer, the chef/owner of the Cub Room, envisioned a comfortable restaurant serving excellent food while providing a sense of peace, relaxation, and refuge from the frenzy of Manhattan. On the Prince Street facade, decorative metal grillwork reflects the industrial history of SoHo, with a contemporary twist. From the bar, the see-and-be-seen atmosphere is enhanced by floor-to-ceiling windows that circle the room. One feels a sense of community in the bar, where Hollywood-style banquettes are covered in antique kilims and low furniture is casually arranged. A low, curved soffit over the bar establishes one of the major visual themes: that of curves, orbs, and globes within rectilinear forms. Through a series of brick arches and a crooked hallway is the main dining room, infused with warm colors via richly colored and textured fabrics. A wall of windows opens onto Sullivan Street, providing light during the day and a sense of theatre in the evening. A cozy fireplace on the interior wall is shared by the private chef's dining room, an inner sanctum adjacent to the kitchen. Throughout, exposed brick and rough edges combine with elegant fabrics and finishes to create visually pleasing contrasts.

timeless

previous page A Carlyle-style banquette is the centerpiece of the room, with its four curved booths.
opposite Warm tones infuse the atmosphere, from jewel-toned tapestry fabrics to rich, secondary tones in
the place settings. above Orbs of light provide a luminous glow in the dining room, where exposed brick
contrasts with elegant fabric and finishes. below The chef's private dining room is a cozy hideaway, a homey
refuge that offers a window onto the kitchen activities.

ARCHITECT/INTERIOR DESIGNER:
Bogdanow Partners Architects P.C.
SQUARE FEET/METERS: *4,500 / 418*
DESIGN BUDGET: *$700,000*
SEATS: *102*
CHECK AVERAGE: *$38*
PHOTOGRAPHER: *© Peter Aaron/Esto*

PINOT BISTRO

STUDIO CITY, CALIFORNIA

Pinot Bistro effectively re-creates the atmosphere of a warm and inviting Parisian bistro in California's San Fernando Valley. To add authenticity to the project, owner Joachim Splichal and designer Cheryl Brantner explored cozy French bistros, flea markets, antique dealers, and salvage yards in Paris. In an extensive renovation, Brantner infused Pinot Bistro with traditional bistro elements—dark wood paneling, ochre walls, a black-and-white tiled floor, banquettes, bistro chairs, and a mirrored bar—plus a second layer of interest. She invokes the spirit of the artists, writers, and celebrities who spent much of their lives in the bars and cafes of Jazz-Age Paris through quotations chalked on mirrors and period photographs perched atop paneled walls. Putting a contemporary spin on flea market finds, Brantner created custom sconces fabricated from bathtub feet, and topped them with antique Parisian flame globes. The bistro is loosely divided into four expansive and comfortable dining areas. Toward the back of the walnut bar area is a private dining room where the designer lets her imagination run wild, paying homage to the surrealist Man Ray, her favorite American artist in Paris. Side walls curve inward at the top, casting light across the giant pair of lips carved into the ceiling—a fanciful touch that leaves an indelible impression.

timeless

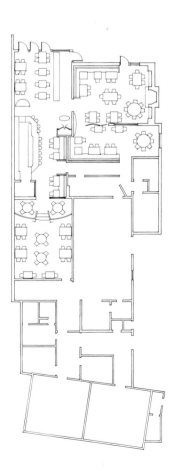

ARCHITECT/INTERIOR DESIGNER:
Brantner Design Associates
SQUARE FEET/METERS: *4,500 / 418*
DESIGN BUDGET: *not disclosed*
SEATS: *140*
CHECK AVERAGE: *$30*
PHOTOGRAPHER: *Douglas Hill*

previous page Warm wooden doors open onto Pinot Bistro's main dining area, which features an open-beam ceiling. left Oversized lips adorn the ceiling and a gargantuan antique clock decorates the back wall of the dining room. top A zigzag tile floor leads to glass paneled doors, adjoining the cafe/bar with the private dining room. above Paying homage to literary greats, quotes are inscribed on mirrors.

VERTIGO
RESTAURANT & BAR

SAN FRANCISCO, CALIFORNIA

The design of Vertigo Restaurant & Bar involved creating a one-of-a-kind restaurant in the heart of downtown San Francisco. The existing 7,800-square-foot structure at the base of the Transamerica Pyramid posed myriad design challenges. The tri-level space, configured around a raised mezzanine, originally had an ominous moat-like appearance. A towering glass ceiling created a flood of natural light, and provided a dizzying view of the Pyramid. The restaurant also lacked American Disability Association access and street presence. To remedy these problems, designers reconfigured the room and bar to allow an integrated, easily serviced main floor with segregated cooking, serving, and dining areas. They extended the mezzanine, creating a contiguous dining space with large, intimate booths set along  a wall of zigzagging glass. Each of the restaurant's three distinct floors makes its own unique design statement. A swirling motif, evident in soffits, fabrics, railings, tile, and booths, softens the imposing scale of the space. A ramp, with inverted copper columns, custom lanterns, and curved lighting track, transports the restaurant's modern architecture down to the street.

timeless

previous page Upon entering the building, guests are struck with the harmonious balance between an imposing architectural structure and a warm and stylish contemporary ambience. left Interior details, rendered in strong, earthy materials, such as wood, copper, and blown glass, harmonize with the concrete beams. above The dining areas combine elements of creativity, such as hot tub-shaped booths, polished wood detailing, and contrasting stripes and solids on upholstery and carpeting. below Copper-mesh screens on the mezzanine ceiling create a shimmering moiré pattern.

ARCHITECT/INTERIOR DESIGNER:
Engstrom Design Group
SQUARE FEET/METERS: *7,800/725*
DESIGN BUDGET: *$1,800,000*
SEATS: *225*
CHECK AVERAGE: *$50*
PHOTOGRAPHERS: *Dennis E. Anderson Photography*
Cesar Rubio Photography

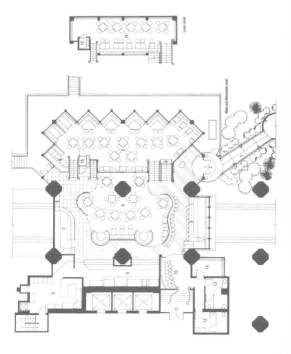

WATER GRILL

LOS ANGELES, CALIFORNIA

Set in the hub of downtown Los Angeles, the designers of Water Grill fused Hollywood panache

with elements of art moderne to create a supper club with an emphasis on bounty from the sea.

At the entrance, guests step through a swag of royal purple velvet, and travel down marble

stairs into a distinguished lounge area, the centerpiece of which is a circular oyster bar piled

high with enticing shrimp, crab, clams, and other raw bar favorites. The walls, paneled with rich

anigré wood, are accented with hand-blown illuminated glass murals depicting

caricatures of the sea. Completing the aura of a haven from the frenetic pace of the

city, a curvilinear, zinc-topped bar offers an ideal spot for a martini. Overhead,

frosted glass lanterns descend from the ceiling. Streamlined ribbed-glass windows

at the perimeter of the bar create both a sense of intimacy and connectedness with

the adjacent dining room. The fluid layout, fanciful wire fish sculptures, subtle

lighting, immense windows, and underwater motif combine to create a feeling of dining in

L.A.'s most chic aquarium.

timeless

previous page Patrons step through a velvet curtain into a sophisticated lounge area, home to a splendid circular raw bar. left Limestone blocks of golden ochre bring external architectural elements inside. The painted cityscape complements the gradations of teal and purple in the ceiling. top Golden wood-paneled walls highlight the colorful, illuminated hand-blown glass murals. above The gleaming, zinc-topped bar is the perfect spot for a cocktail before heading into the adjoining dining room.

ARCHITECT/INTERIOR DESIGNER: *Hatch Design Group*
SQUARE FEET/METERS: *7,950 / 739*
DESIGN BUDGET: *$1,700,000*
SEATS: *195*
CHECK AVERAGE: *$38*
PHOTOGRAPHER: *Martin Fine Photography*

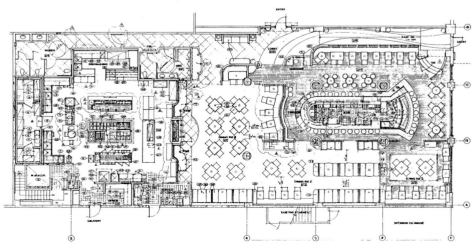

PROVENCE RESTAURANT

WASHINGTON, D.C.

Renowned chef Yannick Cam (owner of Coco Loco) and Savino Recine (owner of Primi Piatti and Coco Loco) combined forces to create Provence Restaurant, a rustic French restaurant inspired by the culture and beauty of Provence. Specializing in the regional cooking of southern France, Provence is an example of how sophistication and simplicity in both decor and cuisine can blend successfully under one roof. Patrons step up flagstone stairs to the wood-burning oven, a hearth that infuses the restaurant's center with warmth. While the restaurant abounds with the aroma of native herbs—rosemary, lavender, fennel, anise, and thyme—patrons' senses are indulged with the colors and textures of the region. Curved, vaulted ceilings provide intimacy and definition to each area, delineating spaces into cozy coves. Limestone walls hold custom-designed wall sconces. Custom ivy ironwork, terra-cotta and stone floors, along with antique Provençal furniture and architectural fragments combine to give Provence Restaurant the aura of a handsome country home.

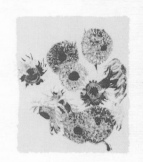

PROVENCE

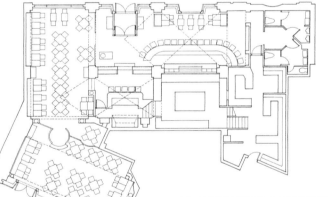

ARCHITECT/INTERIOR DESIGNER:
Adamstein & Demetriou Architecture & Design
SQUARE FEET/METERS: *5,000 / 465*
DESIGN BUDGET: *$780,000*
SEATS: *140*
CHECK AVERAGE: *$60*
PHOTOGRAPHER: © *Theodore Adamstein*

previous page Inspired by
the Provençal countryside, the
wrought-iron vines lead patrons
up to the hearth. left A mottled
terra-cotta floor is juxtaposed
with the limestone bar.
above Limestone and textured
walls, stone floors, curved
ceilings, and antique artifacts
add up to a cozy French setting.
right A sense of accessibility is
achieved through the vaulted
ceilings and open layout.

CAFE SPIAGGIA

CHICAGO, ILLINOIS

The sophisticated and intimate new look of Cafe Spiaggia presents an ideal setting for the traditional yet contemporary cuisine of chef Bartolotta. Created by prominent designer Marve Cooper, the new restaurant showcases contemporary Italian objects of art and design set against a backdrop of pre-Renaissance frescos, inspired by the work of 15th-century artist Andrea Mantegna. The decade-long restoration of Mantegna's 500-year-old frescos, completed in 1993, received major recognition in the art world. Mantegna, court painter to the eminent Gonzaga family, created these murals at Castello di San Giorgio in Mantua, Italy for a room that was used for ceremonial and state affairs. In striking contrast to the 15th-century architectural features at Cafe Spiaggia are the contemporary accents, from light fixtures, to furnishings, to tabletop accents. These elements, coupled with vitrines, are also designed to display the work of modern Italian artists from a wide range of disciplines. The exhibit at the entrance features decorative objects, including stemware and sculptural glass pieces from the collection of Luminaire in Chicago. Other exhibits survey the world of modern art and design, from painting and sculpture, to fashion and contemporary packaging.

timeless

previous page In the north dining room, patrons encounter tall handmade vases by Laura Venini, a fresco entitled, "The Meeting," and colorful jacquard flooring. above & below Framing the banquettes in the north dining room are contemporary pillars, and frescos of ancient Italian landscapes. right The center dining room, which leads into the bar, features cobalt lighting fixtures, cafe tables, and banquettes set along textured walls. next spread Glass vitrines and vases create a gallery setting for artwork from the 20th century.

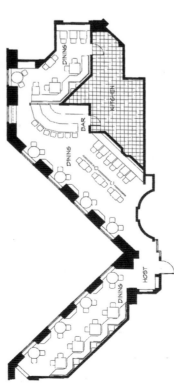

ARCHITECT/INTERIOR DESIGNER: *Marve Cooper Design*
SQUARE FEET/METERS: *1,600 / 149*
DESIGN BUDGET: *$17,500*
SEATS: *83*
CHECK AVERAGE: *$60*
PHOTOGRAPHER: *Mark Ballogg, © Steinkamp/Ballogg Photography*

ANGELO & MAXIE'S STEAKHOUSE

NEW YORK, NEW YORK

A haven for cigar aficionados and carnivores, Angelo & Maxie's Steakhouse was designed as a playful, non-intimidating steakhouse serving up huge portions, fine cigars, stiff drinks, and 1930s New York sensibilities. Designers lined the walls of "Havana Rick's," the restaurant's cigar lounge, with mellow wood panels and Art Deco light fixtures reminiscent of those found in 1930s municipal buildings. In the main dining area, the classic oversized grill chairs feature high backs and comfortable faux-leather upholstery, as do the Hollywood-style booths with head rolls. An open kitchen further energizes the highly charged and lively dining room.

Throughout, original paintings depicting vintage cigar labels and cigar smoking scenes enhance the cigar friendly motif. Overhead, a tin ceiling is bordered with acoustic tiles which do little to suffuse the din. The upper walls are encircled by a lettered frieze that catalogs menu offerings— "Robusto," "Burgundy," "Porterhouse," "Clams"—including classic beef cuts, cigar types, and wine selections in Art Deco lettering.

timeless

previous page The dining room is open and spacious, partitioned with glass room dividers and lit by custom fixtures that re-create a 1930s ambience. left The glass doors which extend to the ceiling molding, open onto the street to allow for natural light and provide an expansive view. above The open kitchen provides a window onto the bustling culinary activities. below The light mahogany bar is stacked to the rafters and is surrounded by welcoming leather-like bar stools.

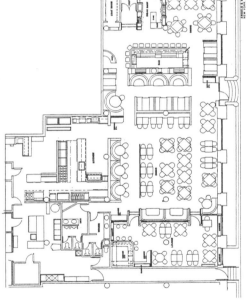

ARCHITECT/INTERIOR DESIGNER:
Morris Nathanson Design
SQUARE FEET/METERS: *6,300 / 585*
DESIGN BUDGET: *$1,000,000*
SEATS: *220*
CHECK AVERAGE: *$38*
PHOTOGRAPHER: *Warren Jagger Photography, Inc.*

ON CANON

BEVERLY HILLS, CALIFORNIA

Memories of Italy's crumbling walls, sun-splashed patios, rich textures, and hidden corners inspired Stanley Felderman's design of the Beverly Hills restaurant, On Canon. Felderman's first moves were to engage the street and to tame the lofty space. He stripped the structure to its bones and broke up the 20-foot glass walls, installing wood framed French windows that open onto a sidewalk terrace. The steel framed atrium windows above are punctuated with branching lights and bowed canopies, giving the room a more inviting sense of scale. A structural column was re-clad  with striated gunmetal-gray plaster to suggest a pivot around which the room and two soffits revolve. A shift in levels was used to create a raised bar and a dining counter that overlooks the main room but is partially screened by a panel of translucent glass. A side patio is treated as an outdoor dining room, and a semi-private corner space caters to parties. Felderman relied on an artisan's skill to create faux finishes that suggest cracked and weathered stained walls. Strong colors are used sparingly, as in the green-stained, wood display cabinets containing flea market finds. Soft tones and wooden floors evoke a Venetian villa, and serve as a backdrop for maple chairs, cherry wood joinery, and subtly striped banquettes.

timeless

previous page Blown-up sketches of Felderman's travels transport patrons to the streets of Italy.
left The column punctures the soffits, revealing a mysterious blue void. Touches of ochre, magenta, and beige provide a pleasing contrast. above The bar and dining areas revolve around the gunmetal structural column topped by spaceship-like soffits that provide visual interest as well as spotlights.
below Colorful tiles and maple chairs enhance the light-filled atmosphere.

ARCHITECT/INTERIOR DESIGNER:
Felderman and Nadel
SQUARE FEET/METERS: *5,000/465*
DESIGN BUDGET: *$1,200,000*
SEATS: *170*
CHECK AVERAGE: *$35*
PHOTOGRAPHER: *Tim Street Porter*

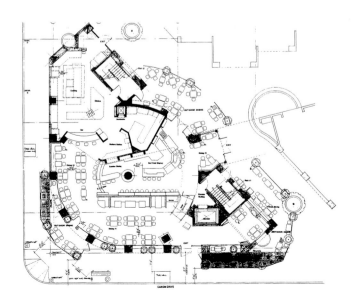

TAMMANY HALL

NEW YORK, NEW YORK

While smartly updated for the '90s, the new Tammany Hall draws heavily on a '30s sensibility for its sophisticated and distinctively contemporary style. The exterior steel and mahogany panels, large glass windows, and wooden blinds suggest a private and intimate interior. The color scheme—stained wood accents and walls painted with old-fashioned, mustard colored milk paint evoke the palette of a film noir movie set that harkens back to the days when Tammany Hall was an old-world social club for Manhattan politicos, goodfellas, and business associates. The room is anchored by a large horseshoe shaped bar which is lit by a chandelier fashioned with actual martini glasses. The bar is surrounded by a textured glass wall, providing a dramatic backdrop to this classic lounge. Serpentine booths padded with comfortable distressed leather offer intimate dining and serve as a divider between the restaurant and the bar. Framed black-and-white archive photos of past New York City mayors imbue the dining room with an otherworldly connection to the Tammany Hall of a bygone era.

timeless

previous page Booths afford a sense of privacy without cutting off the view of other tables. above Serpentine shaped booths snake through the center of the restaurant. Black-and-white photos of previous New York City mayors are juxtaposed against amber walls. right The bar is illuminated by hanging tasseled lights and an unusual chandelier fashioned of actual martini glasses.

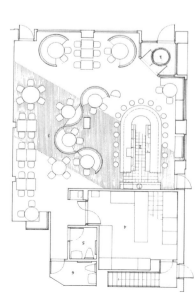

ARCHITECT/INTERIOR DESIGNER:
DiCicco Vinci • Ahn Architects
SQUARE FEET/METERS: *1,385 / 129*
DESIGN BUDGET: *$350,000*
SEATS: *88*
CHECK AVERAGE: *not disclosed*
PHOTOGRAPHER: *© Wade Zimmerman*

L U M A

SANTA MONICA, CALIFORNIA

Luma was conceived as an understated, modern room for alternative fine dining in keeping with the natural, healthy cuisine. The restaurant exudes quiet sophistication through detailing, materials, and above all, lighting. The colors throughout are soft and organic, mirroring those in nature. To create this authentic, subdued effect, all colors were treated—rusted, burnished, honed, sanded or waxed. The neutral palette of finishes includes limestone, American cherry, natural hand-troweled plaster, finely wrought steel, and ivory terrazzo. Running parallel to the entry corridor is a vast vertical plane of opaque glass, the large scale of which sets the

vocabulary of broad baseboards and cove moldings that further exploit the grandeur of the main dining room. Central to the design is a large skylight of sandblasted glass and steel; it functions as a massive light reflector which fills the main dining space with an indirect glow. The shape of industrial windows was duplicated on ceilings and soffits, lending an elegant symmetry to the interior spaces. The design includes an extensive architectural renovation of the pre-existing structure within the newly erected shell, bringing its successful New York formula to Montana Avenue, Santa Monica's premier shopping street.

timeless

previous page The coffered ceiling over the bar adds dramatic height while a segmented, hanging canopy demonstrates spatial dimension.
far left The opaque glass and steel skylight, measuring 14 feet, acts as a light reflector into the expansive dining room below. left & below The Maitre d' desk provides a handsome focal point upon entering, and leads patrons into the bar.

ARCHITECT/INTERIOR DESIGNER:
Branter Design Associates
SQUARE FEET/METERS: *3,650 / 339*
DESIGN BUDGET: *not disclosed*
SEATS: *105*
CHECK AVERAGE: *$40*
PHOTOGRAPHER: *Douglas Hill*

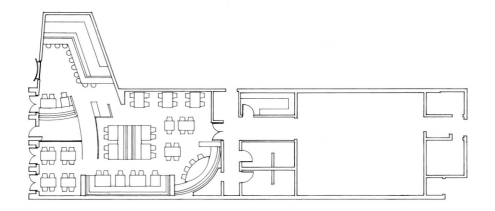

JEAN GEORGES RESTAURANT

NEW YORK, NEW YORK

Jean-Georges Vongerichten's latest culinary sensation is housed in an environment that showcases both his personality and cuisine. The elegant setting, designed by Adam Tihany, is an innovative, engaging restaurant with clean, minimalist lines. But the space presented challenges, such as utilizing the unusual rooms with floor-to-ceiling windows one level above the Columbus Circle promenade; integrating the restaurant with the lobby of the Trump International Hotel and Tower; and making food service available all day. To set the stage, Tihany used a multilevel grid pattern, obvious in the cafe floor (a stunning hand-laid geometric mosaic of marble and terrazzo) and varying square patterned coffered ceilings. Echoing this graphic theme are three silver leaf screens that frame the exhibition kitchen, commanding recessed niches for seating, patterned textiles, and custom china created by Tihany. The grand zinc bar in the cafe and the massive shimmering anigré doors which separate the cafe from the dining room are two of the many impressive architectural elements echoed throughout. The lighting is expertly planned so that it subtly changes in reaction to the light that flows in from many windows.

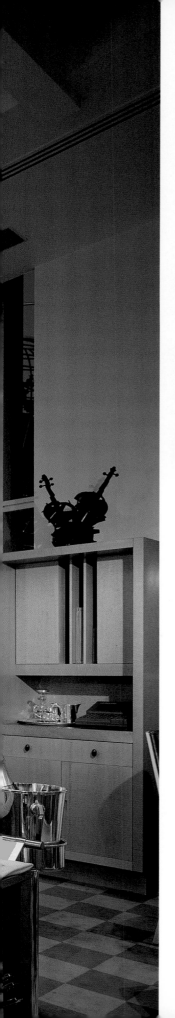

previous page The cozy cafe features light
wood detailing and a customized bar.
left Expansive windows in the main dining area
offer views of Central Park and Columbus Circle.
above An open layout lets diners in the cafe
and lounge areas watch as meals are being prepared in the open kitchen. right A clever glass
wall pocket was designed to house plants, live
flowers, and other seasonal decorations.

INTERIOR DESIGNER:
Adam D. Tihany International, Ltd.
SQUARE FEET/METERS: *5,000 / 465*
DESIGN BUDGET: *not disclosed*
SEATS: *204*
CHECK AVERAGE: *$85*
PHOTOGRAPHER: *Peter Paige*

unconventional

Hudson Club

Eccoqui

Cantaloup

Stir Crazy Cafe

Rococo

California Cafe Bar & Grill

Merchants, NY

T.H.A.I. in Shirlington

Le Cirque 2000

Spiga Ristorante

Zen Palate

Mustard Grille

HUDSON CLUB

CHICAGO, ILLINOIS

Since the original structure of Hudson Club was suggestive of an airplane hangar, designers decided to expand upon the airplane theme, capitalizing on the fluid, horizontal lines of the space and creating one long room that opens onto terraces and dining areas. In keeping with the aeronautical motif, the walls sprouted wings and an oval opening over the bar simulates an airplane window. Along these lines, the sleek, elongated bar features "flights" of wines, dispensed through a 48-foot-long wine keeper that proffers 100 wines by the glass. A sense of

movement was also invoked in the design of chairs and bar stools, employing sections used in airplane fuselage and tail design. Throughout, long horizontal lines curve up and down with flourish and a sense of speed. Hardware for doors and light fixtures curve; railings suggest that they have been bent and molded by ferocious winds. The facade, executed in sheet aluminum with cast-aluminum sconces, frames an oversized egg-shaped window that provides an illuminated view into the restaurant, which fuses classic elements of 1930s design with futuristic industrial materials. The Hudson Club features a small cigar lounge with wingback chairs to top off the nostalgic renaissance.

ARCHITECT/INTERIOR DESIGNER:
Jordan Mozer & Associates, Ltd.
SQUARE FEET/METERS: *10,000 / 929*
DESIGN BUDGET: *$850,000*
SEATS: *270*
CHECK AVERAGE: *$35*
PHOTOGRAPHER: *David Clifton*

previous page The elongated room and seating in meticulous rows was inspired by airplane design.
above The sleek, streamlined bar features a special 48-foot wine storage unit that dispenses more than 100 wines by the glass.   below The whimsical, curved railings were created to provide a sense of movement at high speed.   opposite The exposed rafters are hung with propeller-like fixtures, and "airplane wings" jut out from the walls.

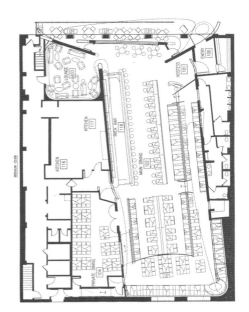

ECCOQUI

BERNARDSVILLE, NEW JERSEY

Transforming an open 5,000-square-foot space adjacent to a supermarket into a sophisticated, yet intimate Tuscan trattoria is nothing less than a remarkable feat, and the designers of Eccoqui met the challenge. To help make the transition from the outdoors, a large domed painting of a cerulean sky greets patrons. Further inside, murals depicting a colorful village evoke the sense of dining alfresco. Soaring columns, coupled with the murals, separate the restaurant into distinct areas. A handsome bar of polished wood accented with crystal panes soars up to the ceiling, stacked high with mineral water, wines, and spirits. Moving into the dining area, patrons step up to a raised level for banquette, booth or cafe seating. The dining room is conceptually divided into two spaces—an interior and exterior—distinguished by different lighting concepts. Walls and ceiling of the "interior" are lit with custom uplights and spotlights aimed at pictures on the walls, while projectors cast light through a foliage screen to create a moonscape at the "exterior." The boundary of this space is defined by custom sconces aimed at the floor. For an artful touch of the country, the designers installed elk horns which jut out from support columns like pieces of sculpture. Eccoqui—a masterful example of how today's designers can successfully blend cutting-edge materials with rustic sensibilities.

unconventional

previous page The designers divided the restaurant without interrupting its flow. At left, the gleaming wood bar overlooks two dining areas as well as the unique illuminated sky dome that sits above the entrance.   left To evoke the sense of dining on the Tuscan hillside, designers commissioned the village mural which spans an entire wall.
above Walls are replete with images of old-world Italy, which are lit by low voltage spotlights.   next spread Even the open kitchen is a delight to the eyes. Designers mixed blue and green tiles, marble countertops, stainless kitchenware, and highly polished wood to create a harmonious textural palette.

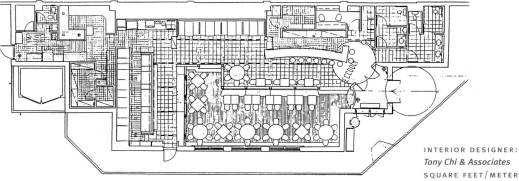

INTERIOR DESIGNER:
Tony Chi & Associates
SQUARE FEET/METERS: *5,000 / 465*
DESIGN BUDGET: *$300,000*
SEATS: *160*
CHECK AVERAGE: *$20*
PHOTOGRAPHER: *Dub Rogers*

CANTALOUP

SÃO PAULO, BRAZIL

An oasis of tranquillity, Cantaloup was erected as a contemporary, nature-inspired respite from the hectic urban pace of São Paulo. Originally home to a small bread factory, the expansive restaurant was conceived with a uniquely open and airy sensibility that has already garnered design awards. This is an exuberant spot where São Paulo's movers and shakers come to indulge their passion for innovative French cuisine and marvelous wine. Patrons enter the restaurant, a combination of two connected though distinct spaces, through wide wooden doors that lead into a lush atrium with sprawling palms, live birds, a sheet of cascading water, and brick patio floors. The main dining room, designed with a hip, cutting-edge motif, is a commanding example of informal chic. It employs openness, and showcases an exposed built-in wine cellar along one wall and an elliptical marble-topped bar along another. The soaring steel ceiling recalls old factories in São Paulo, and is cleverly juxtaposed against more contemporary features, such as polished wood floors, white brick walls, and oversized photographic panels. The custom chairs and banquettes, slipcovered in hues of bright yellow and orange cotton, are pure whimsy, giving a nod to the restaurant's namesake—the cantaloupe melon.

unconventional

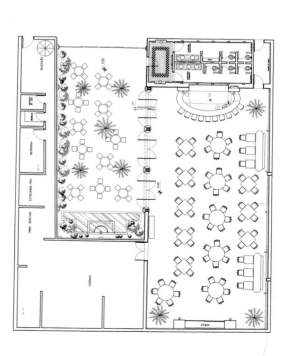

ARCHITECT/INTERIOR DESIGNER:
Arthur de Mattos Casas
SQUARE FEET/METERS: *8,074 / 750*
DESIGN BUDGET: *$1,200,000*
SEATS: *134*
CHECK AVERAGE: *$30*
PHOTOGRAPHER: *Tuca Reinés*

previous page True to the cantaloupe motif, the main dining room uses cool, fresh colors in murals, fabric, and in centerpieces. opposite above The vaulted ceiling is constructed of automated glass panels which open for natural illumination by day and stargazing by night. opposite below The informal tropical patio features colorful mosaic cafe tables surrounded by chairs of straw and iron. above An exposed built-in wine cellar at one end of the room serves as a unique architectural detail.

STIR CRAZY CAFE

NORTHBROOK, ILLINOIS

Following the success of the first Stir Crazy Cafe, the owners decided to open a second "interactive stir-fry" restaurant in the Northbrook Court mall. The cafe offers fresh and light Asian cuisine in a high-energy, interactive dining environment. Restaurant patrons create their own stir-fry dishes by selecting from a variety of fresh noodles, meats, vegetables and sauces, then watch as skilled chefs prepare their meal in a contemporary display kitchen, which is the focal point of the restaurant. To add visual interest, authentic Asian artifacts are nestled on shelving above the open kitchen. The generous use of honey-stained maple throughout, along with numerous other natural materials, make it a fresh and comfortable setting. The space has a harmonious balance of colors and textures including whimsical suspended clouds, decorative ironwork, and serpentine booth railing. A photomural prominently located at one end of the dining room combines spirited graphics with active figures, and is the quintessential representation of the "stir crazy" theme.

unconventional

previous page The main dining area uses natural materials, such as honey-stained maple and iron railings, to create a warm and modern charm. above Paying careful attention to every detail, designers used authentic artifacts, sculpted ironwork, and innovative lighting. right Patrons enter into an expansive bar area that is highlighted with cloud lighting. far right The mural is an original take on the concept of the Japanese screen. next spread Suspended light fixtures at each setting complement the amber glow from above.

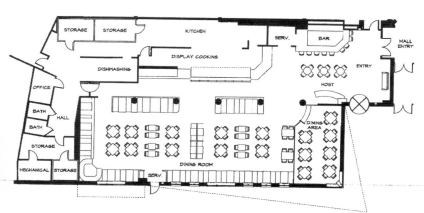

ARCHITECT: *Torchia Associates, Inc.*
INTERIOR DESIGNER: *Marve Cooper Design*
SQUARE FEET / METERS: *5,600 / 520*
DESIGN BUDGET: *$65,000*
SEATS: *200*
CHECK AVERAGE: *$14*
PHOTOGRAPHER: *Mark Ballogg*
© Steinkamp/Ballogg Photography

ROCOCO

PHILADELPHIA, PENNSYLVANIA

History colors the modern elements of Rococo—a huge, glamorous old city restaurant located in the Corn Exchange National Bank. The red brick and white asphalt facade, for example, is embellished with English baroque detailing, including swags, garlands, and small-paned windows. Yet the vastness of the one-and-a-half-story structure, interrupted only by a few sets of elaborate Georgian pilasters and moldings, provided a dramatic backdrop for a fresh approach. To create a heavenly effect, the ceiling, with its garland-encircled coffers and multi-paned skylights, is painted azure with wispy clouds framed in white and offset by soothing yellow walls. Weaving in modern detail, an illuminated metal honeycomb and resin bar snakes through the first floor. To enhance the harmonious environment, designer Floss Barber

incorporated the Asian concept of Feng Shui. Touches of vibrant color lead the eye around the room, including red—an auspicious color according to the dictates of this ancient Eastern philosophy. The main floor houses an open kitchen, the centerpiece of which is an Italian wood-burning brick oven decorated with black granite and Chinese river stones. After dinner, patrons ascend the wrought-iron staircase leading to an austere and chic private smoking lounge appointed with contemporary furnishings, and illuminated with cigar-shaped fixtures.

unconventional

ARCHITECT/INTERIOR DESIGNER:
Floss Barber, Inc.
SQUARE FEET/METERS: *7,500 / 697*
DESIGN BUDGET: *$850,000*
SEATING: *120*
CHECK AVERAGE: *$19*
PHOTOGRAPHERS: *Catherine Tighe Bogert and © Tom Crane*

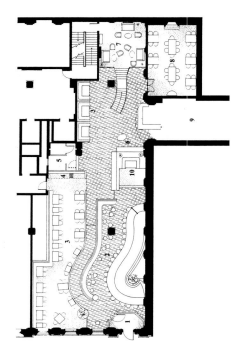

previous page The snaking burlwood dividers, customized banquettes, Georgian-style columns, cobalt accents, and pale yellow walls are repeated throughout the restaurant. To fit within the grand architectural scale of the building, all accents—from windows to flower vases—are created in exaggerated sizes. left The hip, contemporary, and colorful second-story cigar lounge is an example of how designers cleverly fused modern elements within a historic space. above The floor-to-ceiling wine bar is crafted of fine African burlwood. below The curvilinear bar is accented by cobalt blue crushed velvet stools and African burlwood.

CALIFORNIA CAFE BAR & GRILL

LITTLETOWN, COLORADO

Situated in an upscale Colorado shopping mall, California Cafe Bar & Grill is designed in a rustic mountain lodge style—with a twist. Designers infused natural Colorado materials with a California spirit, while avoiding Rocky Mountain clichés. The 10,000-square-foot restaurant is divided into a variety of dining and drinking areas, each with its own distinctive character. The first stop is the bar area, a wood-floored room with curving booths and a vibrant purple soffit  which floats above the maple columns and copper shelves of the 20-foot bar. The room is illuminated by spectacular custom fixtures, some of which are fashioned of wrought iron and blown glass. Across the promenade, an intimate alcove is encircled by iron railings, forged in an abstract naturalistic design. A sloping wall, lined with a curving row of private booths, frames the back of the room. Overhead, a wood-beamed trellis with shimmering mesh fabric creates a sense of enclosure. River rocks abound at the base of the steel-clad fireplace, marking the transition from the bar.

unconventional

previous page One of several alcoves, this dining area is surrounded by custom scrolling wrought-iron railings and towering columns topped with fantasy-inspired lighting. below The 20-foot maple bar and lounge is accented by a large, purple soffit and polished wood floors. right The steel-clad fireplace, surrounded by river boulders, infuses the room with a natural Colorado sensibility. below right A whimsical spider-like lighting fixture and wood-beamed "spider web" archway define the entry vestibule. opposite A clever combination of color, ceiling arches, and custom interior seating creates a bold and contemporary dining spot.

ARCHITECT: *Engstrom Design Group*
INTERIOR DESIGNER: *To Design*
SQUARE FEET/METERS: *9,956 / 926*
DESIGN BUDGET: *$2,300,000*
SEATS: *305*
CHECK AVERAGE *$20*
PHOTOGRAPHER: *© Andrew Kramer*

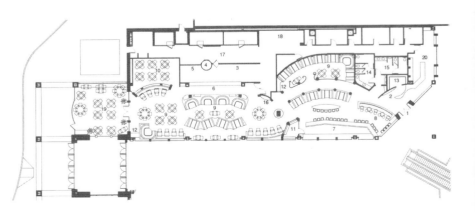

MERCHANTS, NY

NEW YORK, NEW YORK

The design of this hip restaurant, nightspot, and cigar lounge bespeaks luxury, and envelops patrons in its sultry mystique. The slightly retro look of Merchants, NY is achieved through the use of myriad custom materials, including gorgeous wood finishes, rich textiles, decorative painting on walls, elaborate stone flooring, custom wrought-iron grillwork, and bronze shelving behind the bar. Heading downstairs, patrons descend into a pair of intimate wood-paneled lounge rooms that lead to a cigar bar, complete with a working fireplace; here plush lounges and ottomans are scattered in alcoves for a sense of privacy and comfort. On the upper level, a spacious bar serving martinis and premium wines by the glass, is adjacent to an open dining room and private living room lounge. The coffered ceiling reduces noise, and the color scheme—saffron yellow, burnt yellow, deep reds, and natural wood tones—enhances the relaxing environment. In the dining room, the ceiling is lined with sound-absorbent blue velvet and orbs of light. The stairway is lit with fiber optics, as are the ceilings in the downstairs lounges, in which tiny lights twinkle like stars in a blue painted sky.

unconventional

previous page The upstairs integrates a dining room and bar area, so that patrons can easily make the transition from cocktails to dinner. above One of several lounge areas in which custom-crafted seats and banquettes provide an inviting ambience in which to partake of a cigar and nightcap. below Colorful furnishings enliven an alcove in the downstairs lounge. right The main lounge downstairs is a delightful refuge from hectic city living. Coffered ceilings, plush carpeting, and custom furnishings blot out excess noise. next spread The entranceway through the lounges is softly lit by custom cabinetry displaying premium wines, champagnes, and spirits.

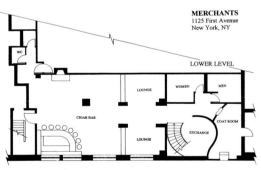

MERCHANTS
1125 First Avenue
New York, NY

LOWER LEVEL

WC

LOUNGE   WOMEN   MEN

CIGAR BAR

COAT ROOM

EXCHANGE

LOUNGE

UPPER LEVEL

LIVING ROOM

BAR

MAIN DINING ROOM

ENTRANCE

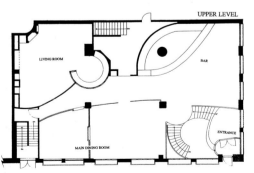

ARCHITECT/INTERIOR DESIGNER:
Bogdanow Partners Architects, P.C.
SQUARE FEET/METERS: *7,000 / 650*
DESIGN BUDGET: *$2,000,000*
SEATS: *190*
CHECK AVERAGE: *not disclosed*
PHOTOGRAPHER: *© Peter Aaron/Esto*

T. H. A. I. IN SHIRLINGTON

SHIRLINGTON, VIRGINIA

Winner of Best Restaurant Ambience in the 1996 International Interior Design Association's regional awards, T.H.A.I. in Shirlington departs from the traditional style associated with Asian restaurants, yet draws from colorful scenes in Thai mythology to create a vibrant dining environment. STUDIOS Architecture took advantage of the natural qualities of the space, layering motifs, paints, and patterns to achieve a uniquely modern effect. Within a somewhat sheltered location in a suburban shopping mall, the design necessitated a strong visual impression in order to lure patrons. The concept of an exposed cubic entrance, composed entirely of glass, offers passersby an unobstructed view into the colorful restaurant. Inside, the low square bar contrasts with the high-sloped, curving planes of the dining room. Walls of various heights, rendered in visually rich colored plasters, are juxtaposed to create a dynamic composition of form and color. Track lighting  highlights artwork and contemporary sconces modifiy the room's scale. The designers built a series of mythological Thai paintings into wall recesses that sweep above the dining room. On this and other walls, textured plaster and gold-leaf interior finishes provide depth.

unconventional

ARCHITECT/INTERIOR DESIGNER:
STUDIOS Architecture
SQUARE FEET/METERS: *3,500/325*
DESIGN BUDGET: *not disclosed*
SEATS: *130*
CHECK AVERAGE: *$40*
PHOTOGRAPHER: *Kenneth M. Wyner*

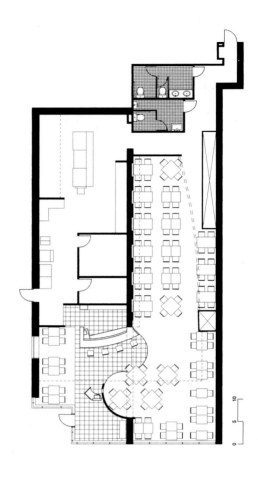

previous page The vibrant and bold color palette in the bar area makes a striking statement and draws patrons further inside. below The high ceiling of the dining room provides a sense of expanse, but it's the clever wall treatments, including the illuminated cutouts and recessed prints, that prompt diners to gaze upward. right Custom-designed tables feature subtle elements of Thai decor.

LE CIRQUE 2000

NEW YORK, NEW YORK

Breathing new life into one of the most famous restaurants of all time, Adam D. Tihany, the premier restaurant designer of the decade, masterminded a new Le Cirque to transport restaurateur Sirio Maccioni's famed dining emporium into the next millennium. Instead of re-creating the landmarked interiors of historic Villard houses in an elegant period piece, Tihany first restored architectural features to their original splendor. He then added a heavy dose of carnival, showcased in decorative elements and furnishings reminiscent of the Cirque du Soleil. Patrons slip through a tent of brightly colored silk into a New Age fantasyland for dinner under the big top. Against ornate walnut paneling in the Grill Room, are bright red and yellow banquettes, and in the marbled hall, vividly colored club chairs are a whimsical lounging spot. The main dining room is occupied by tall, one-armed chairs with buttons down the backs,

fashioned after clown costumes, while the carpet is a literal riot of color, complete with circus rings. The crowning glory is the futuristic bar, with massive torchieres and suspended neon rings—Tihany's solution to illuminating the room without affixing lights to the Renaissance-style ceilings. Like a high-wire act, a suspended clock slides over patrons' heads. How does Tihany justify the fusion of decor? "It's like putting a Ferrari in an old palazzo," he says.

previous page The reception hall features a billowy silk tent. The carpet, a mass of colorful designs and swirls, evokes the aura of theatrical spotlights. opposite The grand staircase in the main hall showcases the restaurant's multi-million-dollar restoration. left Green Mohair velvet upholstery provide spirited accents in the marbled main hall. below The Grill Room boasts red and yellow, harlequin-inspired furnishings.

ARCHITECT:
Harman Jablin Architects
INTERIOR DESIGNER:
Adam D. Tihany, International Limited
SQUARE FEET/METERS: *15,000 / 1,394*
DESIGN BUDGET: *not disclosed*
SEATS: *220*
CHECK AVERAGE: *$65*
PHOTOGRAPHER: *Peter Paige*

previous spread Architectural details are accented by boldly colored chairs and couches in the Madison Room. opposite A clock travels back and forth on a tightrope within the enormous ringed neon sculpture in the bar. Giant torchieres reach up to the ornate gilded ceiling—a jewel in and of itself. above Traditional details such as gilded moldings and ceiling fresco take center stage in the drawing room. left The Library Banquet Room boasts a richly detailed, vaulted ceiling.

SPIGA
RISTORANTE

SCARSDALE, NEW YORK

The design team for Spiga set out to create an open, 200-seat Italian fantasy restaurant infused with light, color, and a sense of playfulness. The first order of business was gutting a cramped franchise eatery, and opening the space to the rafters. The designers immediately established a dream-like mood, adorning the outdoor canopies with bright stars and moons, and carrying the celestial theme into the restaurant, where  constellations crop up on banquettes and on the ceiling in the form of custom, recessed, star and moon light fixtures. The adjoining bar and restaurant are distinguished from one another with low mahogany panels and a series of leaning arches glazed in hues of burnt amber, terra cotta, and plum. A changing selection of fresh Tuscan antipasti is displayed along the copper-topped bar and enhanced by a series of pendant lights and encased glass. The exposed freestanding pizza oven, surrounded by a copper canopy, allows guests to marvel as gourmet pizzas are created before their eyes. Overhead, an imaginary townscape is painted in the perimeter dining area that rises to a peak in the restaurant's center. As Spiga's grand focal point, the mural draws upon the art and history of the Italian countryside.

unconventional

previous page The hand-painted chiaroscuro mural recalls the Italian countryside. opposite The designers used brightly-colored walls, an open floor plan, and gigantic angled arches to draw the eye around the room. above & left Celestial lighting above the bar and open oven area simulates an evening sky.

ARCHITECT/INTERIOR DESIGNER:
Haverson Architecture & Design, P.C.
SQUARE FEET/METERS: *7,000 / 650*
DESIGN BUDGET: *$600,000*
SEATS: *175*
CHECK AVERAGE: *$25*
PHOTOGRAPHER: *© Paul Warchol*

NINTH AVENUE

UNION SQUARE

BROADWAY

ZEN PALATE

NEW YORK, NEW YORK

Inspired by Buddhist temples and shrines, the design concept at all three Zen Palate vegetarian restaurants is based on harmonious interlocking and free-flowing geometric spaces which create a "Zen-like" experience. The 9th Avenue installation, the first of three, is an attractive bistro setting with saffron-colored walls and a pale-blue, faux-marble ceiling that evokes peace and tranquillity when guests pass through the fortress-like metal studded doors. French cafe chairs, and subdued lighting add an air of informality. At Union Square, the largest of the trio, dining is available on three floors, partitioned only by giant mahogany beams. The ground level highlights an open kitchen and counter service, while the upper levels offer a more calm and relaxed environment, complete with a tatami room and tea service. The mahogany tea bar provides a showcase for colorful teapots and artifacts, as well as low tables surrounded with floor pillows. The inspiration for the newest Zen Palate on the Upper West Side is an old Asian alleyway that fronts onto bustling Broadway. As in its sister restaurants, it features subdued lighting and wood walls. Here, windows serve as novel partitions between dining areas and the intimate setting fulfills the designers' vision—to provide a window onto the comings and goings of neighborhood residents, as well as a refuge for diners.

unconventional

ZEN PALATE 9TH AVE.
INTERIOR DESIGNER:
Tony Chi & Associates
SQUARE FEET/METERS: *3,000 / 279*
DESIGN BUDGET: *$400,000*
SEATS: *200*
CHECK AVERAGE: *$20*
PHOTOGRAPHER: *Dub Rogers*

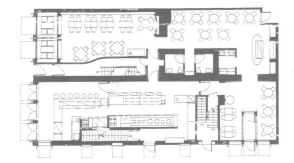

above At the 9th Avenue location, Asian 'tea art' services in private tatami rooms serve up to four people. left Metal-studded doors partition the bar and dining area. below Muted walls lit by custom sconces create a mellow ambience.

above At the Union Square location, a dark mahogany tea bar stands in striking contrast to soothing saffron-yellow walls. below left Buddha keeps a watchful eye over an informal Asian bistro dining area. below center A mahogany staircase leads to upper-level dining alcoves. below right A tea bar with poured concrete floors is based on the concept of Buddhist temples, in which natural materials unify multiple levels.

ZEN PALATE UNION SQUARE
INTERIOR DESIGNER:
Tony Chi & Associates
SQUARE FEET/METERS: *8,000 / 743*
DESIGN BUDGET: *$800,000*
SEATS: *250*
CHECK AVERAGE: *$20*
PHOTOGRAPHER: © *1993 Norman McGrath*

above & opposite below At Zen Palate Broadway, dark mahogany chairs and light wooden furnishings provide warm Asian accents illuminated by decorative hanging lanterns.

ZEN PALATE BROADWAY
INTERIOR DESIGNER:
Tony Chi & Associates
SQUARE FEET/METERS: *1,800 / 167*
DESIGN BUDGET: *$450,000*
SEATS: *100*
CHECK AVERAGE: *$20*
PHOTOGRAPHER: © 1996 Norman McGrath

above Narrow, elongated windows were installed to allow patrons a view onto the comings and goings of Broadway. At night, radiant indoor lamps set off an inviting glow.

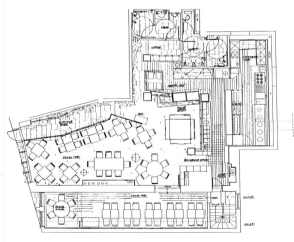

MUSTARD GRILLE

MISSISSAUGA, ONTARIO

Mustard Grille was designed to reflect an upbeat atmosphere reminiscent of the roaring '20s. While the emphasis of the restaurant was on high-quality food, the owners sought a design that was fresh, artistic, and comfortable. A jazz-oriented palette of vibrant colors creates a feeling of exuberance, which is mirrored by the ambience and the food. To maintain the focus on quality dining, an open kitchen and food preparation area, featuring a long chef's table on a raised central platform, adds to the entertainment aspect of the restaurant. Custom-designed faux finishes, wall treatments, and hand-painted murals depicting 1920s jazz players, explode with vibrancy. Several floor finishes are combined and some seating areas are raised to achieve a tiered effect. Purple archways give the illusion of three dining areas instead of one. To accommodate large groups, a private wine tasting/dining room, centered around a communal table and customized wine storage units, provides a haven for private dining. In 1996, a jazz club/lounge was added with plush, colorful velvet upholstery, textured faux wall finishes, and flowing silk drapery, complementing the sights and sounds of cool jazz. The space's sensual, flowing curves are indicative of the music borne within, while its lively color scheme and cozy oversized furnishings leave guests feeling relaxed yet energized.

unconventional

previous page Bluesy colors of mustard, green, and purple are blended with jazz-hot red. above Cocktail stools and asymmetrical tables are scattered throughout the lounge, providing myriad places to mix, mingle or enjoy the sounds of a jazz trio. right The large table, set against the backdrop of a hand-painted mural, is perfect for private parties and wine-testing dinners. far right The refrigeration cases and open kitchen are integrated into the design and flow of the restaurant.

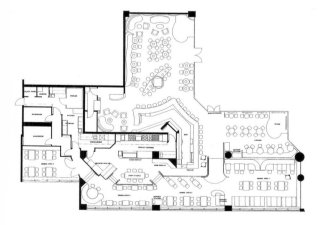

ARCHITECT/INTERIOR DESIGNER:
Martin Hirschberg Design Associates, Ltd.
SQUARE FEET/METERS: *5,100 / 474*
DESIGN BUDGET: *$250,000*
SEATS: *182*
CHECK AVERAGE: *$75*
PHOTOGRAPHER: *Richard Johnson, Interior Images*

Laissez-Faire

I Cugini Ristorante

Regata Cafe

Girasole Ristorante & Bar

Caffe Bellissimo

Raku – an Asian Diner

Graffiti's Italian Eatery & Saloon

Republic

Spezzo Ristorante

Tosca

Del Dente

Rain

I CUGINI RISTORANTE

SANTA MONICA, CALIFORNIA

Santa Monica's I Cugini Ristorante is a cozy trattoria that merges traditional Italian flavor with 20th-century design. In direct contrast to the contemporary limestone facade, the rustic interior of this 8,000-square-foot space combines elements of Italian decor—marble, terrazzo, granite, scrolled iron, and heavy woven tapestries—to create an authentic Mediterranean ambience. Historical details are complemented by contemporary touches, such as walls painted with a stone-like faux finish and large-scale parquet flooring. Hand-painted Manet-style murals above the wainscoted walls adorn the serpentine booths, while delicately painted sheaths of wheat and flowers crown the barrel-vaulted ceiling. By day, the attached outdoor patio affords natural light as well as a spectacular ocean view. At night, custom iron and alabaster chandeliers provide a soft glow. The exhibition-style cookline, wood-burning oven, attached market, and bakery put patrons in the center of the action. By giving weathered materials a modern flair, the designers created a lively European bistro in the heart of Santa Monica.

laissez-faire

previous page The hand-painted domed ceiling and antique light fixtures create a warm ambience at I Cugini. left The marble-topped counter area provides a window onto the preparations and provisions. above The scrolled ironwork and parquet floors complement the array of Mediterranean-inspired touches.

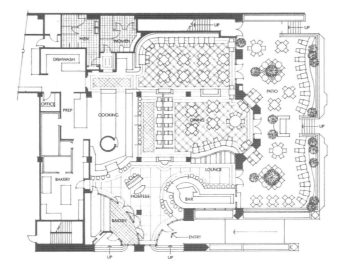

ARCHITECT/INTERIOR DESIGNER:
Hatch Design Group
SQUARE FEET/METERS: *8,000/743*
DESIGN BUDGET: *$1,600,000*
SEATS: *275*
CHECK AVERAGE: *$27*
PHOTOGRAPHER:
© 1996 Milroy & McAleer Photography

REGATA CAFE

TEL AVIV, ISRAEL

Regata Cafe, an exuberant, informal dining spot designed by Adam D. Tihany, overlooks the bustling waterfront and the mesmerizing waters of the Mediterranean. Inspired by gondola races on the Venetian Lagoon, Regata Cafe deftly captures the exhilarating spirit of sailing. Sun and sea are reflected in the yellow and blue palette as well as in the undulating "flying waves" ceiling and light shades, striped nautical chairs, and vibrant multicolored terrazzo-topped tables. Even the floor, tiled in high-gloss marble, re-creates the look of sand. As in several other Tihany designs, the room is open, bright, and features a variety of focal points. The exhibition kitchen and wood-burning oven, for instance, underscore the visible, made-to-order food concept by bringing food preparation into full view. In keeping with the theme, a unique serving counter perched over a simulated indoor swimming pool is a popular spot for a quick bite. Panoramic windows shaded by canvas blinds frame the spectacular beachfront view. As a final touch, all food is served on custom designed "Archipiatti" dinnerware, a composition of color and geometric shapes designed to complement the seaside theme.

right A riot of mixed colors, geometric patterns and Mediterranean-inspired details evoke a relaxed and festive air. below Sunny yellow and blue sails frame the bar, and continue the "flying wave" motif showcased throughout the main dining area. below right "Poolside" seating tops off Regata Cafe's sophisticated take on fast food.

ARCHITECT/DESIGNER:
Adam D. Tihany International, Ltd.
SQUARE FEET/METERS: *5,000 / 465*
DESIGN BUDGET: *not disclosed*
SEATS: *175*
CHECK AVERAGE: *not disclosed*
PHOTOGRAPHER:
Maurizio Mercato/WALD s.r.l.

GIRASOLE
RISTORANTE & BAR

PHILADELPHIA, PENNSYLVANIA

Inspired by the restaurant's name (*Girasole* means sunflower in Italian), the designers transformed a dark narrow space on a nondescript city block in the heart of Philadelphia into a sunny Italian bistro. They created a light, open space by knocking out walls and gutting all existing architecture—except the kitchen. A custom, curvilinear, steel and marble bar emblazoned with bright yellow jacquards was placed at the glass front to attract attention from the sidewalk. Distinctive hanging fixtures, an extravagant display of glittering bottles on glass shelves, shrewdly located mirrors, and a tremendous bouquet of sunflowers in a colorful Mexican urn create an immediate impact. The marble, wood-burning pizza oven, and the Macchiavelli terra-cotta floor tiles were imported from Italy by the client. In the dining area, custom inlaid marble tabletops sit on wrought iron bases, and are surrounded by chairs that were reupholstered to match new banquette seating. Walls were textured and painted to simulate sun-dappled Italian stucco. Large painted photographic portraits of sunflowers, and replicas of 15th-century column capitals from a palace in Urbino hang on the wall above the banquette.

laissez-faire

previous page Large, painted, photographic portraits were commissioned to emphasize the sunflower theme. opposite Billowy, cloud-like light fixtures enhance the natural ambience emanating from the simulated Italian stucco walls. left Shades of yellow and red earth tones throughout the dining room complement terra-cotta floor tiles. below left Perched above the banquette are decorative replicas of 15th-century column capitals from a palace in Urbino. below The custom, marble-topped bar was strategically placed near large windows to attract attention from the sidewalk.

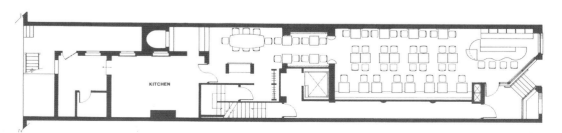

ARCHITECT (INTERIOR): *Floss Barber, Inc.*
SQUARE FEET/METERS: *1,850 / 172*
DESIGN BUDGET: *$500,000*
SEATING: *55*
CHECK AVERAGE: *$25*
PHOTOGRAPHERS: *© Jeffrey Totaro, © Matt Wargo*

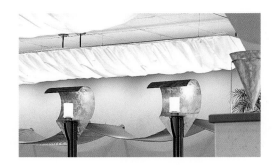

CAFFE BELLISSIMO

SPRINGFIELD, PENNSYLVANIA

By tapping into the wealth of Italian culture—past and present—the designers of Caffe Bellissimo incorporated the best elements of traditional hospitality into the context of a contemporary Italian restaurant. Bentel & Bentel Architects used the finest natural materials to transform the space, and with an innovative take on the existing structure, captured the warmth of an authentic trattoria in the heart of Pennsylvania. The restaurant re-creates an Italian courtyard, with an adjoining narrow space reminiscent of the quaint streets of a Mediterranean village. Patrons enter through the low broad arches and wood-beamed ceilings of the loggia, where the bar and take-out provide an obliging welcome. The essence of the design—handcraftsmanship—is immediately palpable at the bar, constructed of granite, copper, and cherry. In the dining room, cloth chandeliers glow like sunlit clouds over copper-rubbed ash wood tables, and a column in the center was transformed into an  abstract "tree". An exposed, tile and copper-clad oven is the focal point of the room, enabling guests to view pizza chefs in action. A terrace seating area surrounded by low travertine and copper walls completes the stimulating imagery of Italy.

laissez-faire

previous page The entry vestibule is a rich example of the architect's use of natural materials, from the wood-beamed ceilings to copper accents. left Custom designed lampposts along with cloth chandeliers re-create a sense of outdoor illumination. above Handcrafted pizzas and breads are prepared in full view of diners at the tile and copper-clad oven. below left Vine-like lighting fixtures complement the rich earth tones of travertine walls and cherry wood bar stools. below right Striped awnings draped above banquettes loosely reinterpret the form of an Italian courtyard.

ARCHITECT/INTERIOR DESIGNER:
Bentel & Bentel Architects
SQUARE FEET/METERS: *5,600 / 520*
DESIGN BUDGET: *$500,000*
SEATS: *177*
CHECK AVERAGE: *$16*
PHOTOGRAPHER: *© Arch Photo, Inc./Eduard Hueber*

RAKU
AN ASIAN DINER

WASHINGTON, D.C.

A hybrid of the Japanese and Chinese noodle bar, Raku-an Asian Diner serves innovative fresh food in an exciting and fast-paced setting. The restaurant's design, which was awarded the 1996 American Institute of Architects Award for Interior Architecture, draws on the rich imagery of the East to complement the high-energy food concept. Traditional forms and symbols were transformed into a contemporary language that is tactile and sensual, yet whimsical. There is a strong emphasis furthermore, on natural materials—metal, stone, wood, and paper. This play between the man-made and the natural, the traditional and the playful, forms the basis of the design. The resulting structure revolves around a massive copper hearth and grill set against red-lacquer paneling and glowing shoji screens. A curvilinear stone and wood dining counter sits on patterned slate floors. Overhead, the ceiling is dominated by giant bamboo chopsticks and vibrant oversized parasols, while custom sconces and large video monitors add visual excitement.

previous page The restaurant achieves a harmonious blend of natural elements—wood and slate floors, brick and stone walls, and beamed ceilings. above The striking overhead parasols bring an infusion of color into an oasis of natural hues. Natural light from windows brightens up the space. right The curvilinear bar is set against a wall of intense red lacquer.

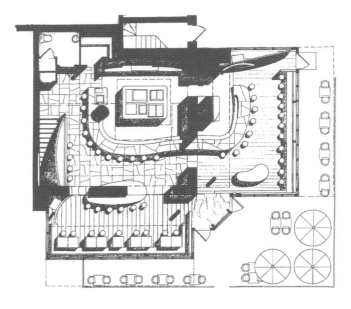

ARCHITECT/INTERIOR DESIGNER:
Adamstein & Demetriou Architecture
SQUARE FEET METERS: *2,500 / 232*
DESIGN BUDGET: *$600,000*
SEATS: *64*
CHECK AVERAGE: *$13*
PHOTOGRAPHER: *© Theodore Adamstein*

GRAFFITI'S ITALIAN EATERY & SALOON

MISSISSAUGA, ONTARIO

At Graffiti's, a warm Mediterranean feeling that captures the mood of an Italian street "festa" is created through extensive use of wood, steel, and imported tile and ceramics. The design provides for maximum display cooking, featuring a large built-in flaming pizza oven, an open salad and pasta station, and an eating counter where guests can have a bite while watching the action. To complement the Italian food and festival atmosphere, the background music features old-time crooners from days gone by. Northern Italian cracked-stucco walls, wood stained a dark red Chianti, terra-cotta tiles, and wrought-iron grillwork further enhance the motif. Adding to the restaurant's charm are country street scenes, depicted in oil murals, and painted tabletops, each lovingly created by local art students. Overhead beer garden string lights, custom street lamps, fabric canopies, and paved stones also play upon the festival theme. An Italian rococo chandelier and gaudy gold table lamps are mounted upside down over booths in the style of pendant lights. The bar is particularly unique, with high ceilings and an ample display of spirits running the 50-foot length of the bar.

previous page The bar area features cafe tables, banquettes, and a 50-foot bar lined with spirits. left The main dining area pivots around the canopied pizza oven, colorful checkered tile, striped awnings, and custom banquettes. above To create a relaxed street festival feeling, the ceilings are strung with beer garden lights, and the tables are topped with hand-painted designs. below Painted murals throughout the restaurant are framed with Italian tile.

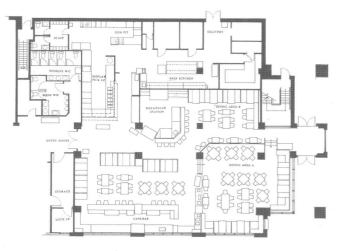

ARCHITECT/INTERIOR DESIGNER: *Cricket Design Co.*
SQUARE FEET/METERS: *6,000 / 557*
DESIGN BUDGET: *$650,000*
SEATS: *175*
CHECK AVERAGE: *$15*
PHOTOGRAPHER: *Richard Johnson/Interior Images*

R E P U B L I C

NEW YORK, NEW YORK

Simplicity translates into sleek minimalism at Republic—one of the most stylish noodle emporiums in New York City. Chic yet elegant, the designers of Republic captured an ultramodern atmosphere that quietly conveys the fresh uniqueness of gourmet food served up quickly. Studio GAIA met the challenge of transforming a long, narrow space, by creating a bar and open kitchen at the entrance of the restaurant. The elongated area now serves as an enticing entry, leading patrons into the main dining room which was raised for visibility. The dining area features pale blue and green walls, contrasted by lively orange borders and bar stools which are enhanced by theatrical lighting. From the arch-shaped long bluestone bar, as well as dining tables, guests can enjoy the main stage area—the open kitchen. A collective effort of an innovative group of veteran restaurateurs, the Republic concept combines cooking methods from Vietnam, Malaysia, China, Thailand and Japan. Black and white photographs of figures draped in noodles combine with Asian elements, such as Japanese paper hung on metal cables, for a result that is pure harmony.

laissez-faire

previous page An inviting bar with its long, curved counter leads patrons into the main dining room. left Photographs of figures draped in noodles and a soft strip of Japanese paper hung from above create Republic's unique aura. top Egalitarianism pervades the main dining hall, with its communal style seating on solid birch tables and benches. above Patrons can sit at the open kitchen, or step up the raised platform for seating in the dining room.

ARCHITECT/DESIGNER: *Studio GAIA*
SQUARE FEET/METERS: *3,800 / 353*
DESIGN BUDGET: *$850,000*
SEATS: *160*
CHECK AVERAGE: *$15*
PHOTOGRAPHER *Nagamitsu Endo Photography*

SPEZZO RISTORANTE

RICHMOND HILL, ONTARIO

Upon entering Spezzo, diners are immediately aware that they are part of something special: flickering candles, flowing ironwork, warm colors, and rich textures entice the senses. Located in a suburban area, Spezzo was renovated to re-create a dining experience comparable to that found in Milan and Rome. Catering to those who appreciate good food, fine wine, and cigars, the interior of this upscale Italian restaurant matches the sophisticated menu while providing a relaxed, comfortable dining experience. The rustic country ambience was created by using aged, faux finishes in neutral, taupe, rust, and olive green. Rich cherry wood and dark slate-like tiles add to the earthy sensuousness of the space, as do the custom fireplace and the circular banquettes. Organic shaped wrought iron flows like vines in abstract curves, decorating the entire space. To emphasize the importance of  the food, a large chef's preparation table, antipasto station, and pizza oven were brought center stage. To indulge every sense, the creation of an open lounge/bar area allows customers to walk only a few steps to enjoy an after-dinner drink and live jazz.

previous page The open layout creates a unified experience, putting the bar and lounge area within sight of the main dining areas. above Spezzo embodies a fusion of rustic elements shown here in the blazing hearth, tiled flooring, and exhibition kitchen. right Custom ironwork appears in many guises: on the chairs and bar stools, as well as on the whimsical decorative sculptures throughout. far right A circular banquette allows patrons to sit back and view the city skyline from French doors.

ARCHITECT/INTERIOR DESIGNER:
Martin Hirschberg Design Associates, Ltd.
SQUARE FEET/METERS: *5,000 / 465*
DESIGN BUDGET: *not disclosed*
SEATS: *200*
CHECK AVERAGE: *$30*
PHOTOGRAPHER: *Richard Johnson/Interior Images*

TOSCA

HINGHAM, MASSACHUSETTS

Tosca's owners, a thirty-something couple who owned a sandwich shop, wanted to open a theatrical Northern Italian restaurant with a focus on wood grilled foods. As such, the designers set out to create an open kitchen, displaying the cooking line, wood fired pizza ovens, rotisseries, and food preparation areas, thereby bringing the sights, sounds, and scents of the kitchen into the dining room. The site was originally a working granary mill, then a restaurant space that went through several incarnations. The former restaurant had mezzanine seating and offices, which the designers removed to expose original wood rafters. These natural supports and brick walls became a major element of the design. To tie in

with the natural decor, designers installed a custom wood floor and rimmed it with shards of multicolored tile for easy maintenance. Simple furniture, rag painted walls, and varied low-level lighting create a cozy ambience throughout. Tabletop lamps, for instance, provide a sense of intimacy, while large custom chandeliers of multicolored glass suggest high art. Finally, the open bar, stained a rich mahogany, provides dramatic tension with the adjoining dining area, and a place to people-watch and enjoy appetizers while awaiting a table. Painted on canvas and suspended on theater batons above the bar, is an adaptation of one of the original curtains used in the staging of the opera *Tosca*, the restaurant's namesake.

previous page In keeping with the theme, walls are adorned with antique opera posters and the bar is framed by stage curtains.
left To ensure that the wait staff is on the floor and available to customers at all times, designers created an open storage unit that brings all utensils and dinnerware to the front of the restaurant. **above** Tabletop lamps and low-level lighting emit a cozy warmth.
next spread The open layout provides patrons with a full view of the wood fired ovens, bar, and dining rooms.

ARCHITECT/INTERIOR DESIGNER:
Morris Nathanson Design
SQUARE FEET/METERS: *5,600 / 520*
DESIGN BUDGET: *$780,000*
SEATS: *200*
CHECK AVERAGE: *$35*
PHOTOGRAPHER: *Warren Jagger Photography, Inc.*

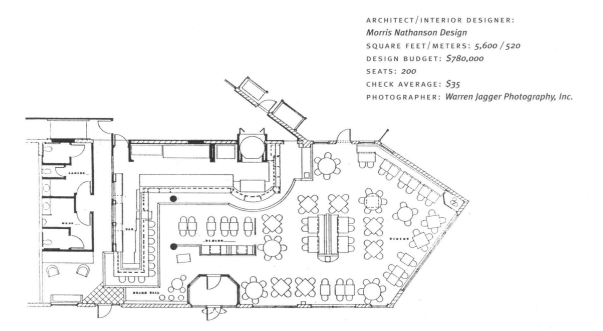

DEL DENTE

KITCHENER, ONTARIO

An adjunct to the Charcoal Steak House in a mid-sized Ontario manufacturing town, Del Dente's renovation was meant to bring fun, casual, current, yet non-intimidating Italian dining to local residents. First, the designers at Cricket Design Company Inc. set out to provide a casual atmosphere with heightened visual stimuli and increased interaction between guests and staff. To accomplish this, they arranged the restaurant so that each

space displays wine, food, and desserts, as well as a view of the open kitchen. In the main dining area, each tabletop was custom-painted by a local college art student, showcasing a spectrum of styles. An open bakery area was added to introduce the scent of fresh baked breads, which are cooked and served in terra-cotta pots and presented with a range of flavored butters. In addition, family photos, Italian street posters, and other memorabilia create a convivial atmosphere. On a strict budget, the designer successfully implemented the renovation to create this cozy Mediterranean-inspired dining spot.

previous page The overall atmosphere of the dining room is festive, open, and casual, with chalkboards featuring nightly specials, and a view into the bar and kitchen. opposite A colorful gallery of art styles adorns the tabletops. left The bar is illuminated by custom, wrought-iron fixtures and surrounded by classic swivel stools. below Cafe chairs and tables, with red-and-white checkered tablecloths, complete the intimate setting. bottom The focal point for diners is the open bakery with pizza ovens, which turns out an array of wonderful fresh-baked breads and enticing aromas.

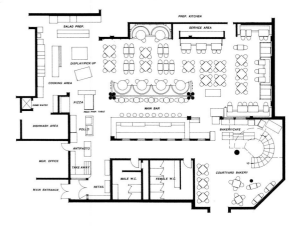

INTERIOR DESIGNER:
Cricket Design Company Inc.
SQUARE FEET/METERS: *6,200/576*
DESIGN BUDGET: *$500,000*
SEATS: *220*
CHECK AVERAGE: *$17*
PHOTOGRAPHER: *Kwoi*

R A I N

NEW YORK, NEW YORK

Just as the menu fuses cuisine from Malaysia, Thailand, and Vietnam, Rain mixes design elements from Southeast Asia and Manhattan. The result is a Pan-Asian dining experience with decidedly urban flair. The designers set the mood with a color palette of saffron, burnt yellow, and deep red that suggests a warm Southeast Asian climate. The venue is peppered with natural wood accents softened by a delicate lighting scheme of cut-paper silhouettes over light boxes. Faced with an oversized bar area and imposing structural columns that could not be moved, the architects divided the original space by scaling down the bar, creating a cozy lounge area, and building a raised dining platform with Japanese-style booths and a second dining area framed by delicate Asian screens. The addition of a gazebo in the bar area created a space for comfortable settees and relaxed cocktail seating. Cushioned rattan sofas and chairs furnish an inviting lounge, and a hand-painted oriental runner leads patrons from the bar and lounge into the interior of the restaurant. Funky New York antiques and Asian furnishings complete the fusion of styles.

previous page While waiting for a table, guests can either relax on a stool at the bar or on an upholstered settee under the gazebo.
left and below Patrons have the option of dining in either of two areas—each offers a unique mood. One is painted in light saffron with pale wood Japanese-style booths; the other, with a more somber ambience, is outfitted with ochre walls and dark accents.
above A hand-painted runner transports guests into the restaurant.

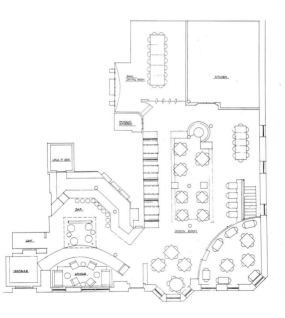

ARCHITECT/INTERIOR DESIGNER:
Bogdanow & Partners Architects
SQUARE FEET/METERS: *2,800 / 260*
DESIGN BUDGET: *$85,000*
SEATS: *125*
CHECK AVERAGE: *$50*
PHOTOGRAPHER: *Robert Vance Blosser*

RESTAURANTS

Angelo & Maxie's Steakhouse
233 Park Avenue
New York, New York 10003
United States
Tel: (212) 220-9200
Fax: (212) 220-9209

Cafe Spiaggia
980 North Michigan Avenue
Chicago, Illinois 60611
United States
Tel: (312) 280-2750
Fax: (312) 943-8560

Caffe Bellissimo
1001 Baltimore Turnpike
Springfield, Pennsylvania 19808
United States
Tel: (610) 328-2300

California Cafe Bar & Grill
8505 Park Meadows Center Drive
Littleton, Colorado 80124
United States
Tel: (303) 649-1111
Fax: (303) 649-1731

Cantaloup
Rua Manoel Guedes 474
São Paulo, São Paulo
Brazil 01410-002
Tel: (55) 11-866-6445
Fax: (55) 11-820-9884

Cub Room
131 Sullivan Street
New York, New York 10012
United States
Tel: (212) 677-4100

Del Dente
2980 King Street East
Kitchener, Ontario N2A-1A9
Canada
Tel: (519) 893-6570
Fax: (519) 693-7072

Eccoqui
107 Route 202
Bernardsville, New Jersey 07924
United States
Tel: (908) 221-0040

Girasole Ristorante & Bar
1305 Locust Street
Philadelphia, Pennsylvania 19106
United States
Tel: (215) 985-4659
Fax: (215) 985-0540

Graffiti's Italian Eatery & Saloon
262 Carlingview Drive
Mississauga, Ontario M9W-5G1
Canada
Tel: (416) 213-1300
Fax: (416) 674-3088

Hudson Club
504 North Wells Street
Chicago, Illinois 60610
United States
Tel: (312) 467-1947

I Cugini Ristorante
1501 Ocean Avenue
Santa Monica, California 90401
United States
Tel: (310) 451-4595
Fax: (310) 451-9026

Jean Georges Restaurant
One Central Park West
New York, New York 10023
United States
Tel: (212) 299-3900
Fax: (212) 299-3914

Le Cirque 2000
455 Madison Avenue
New York, New York 10022
United States
Tel: (212) 303-7788
Fax: (212) 303-7712

Luma
1323 Montana Avenue
Santa Monica, California 90403
United States

Merchants, NY
1125 First Avenue
New York, New York 10021
United States
Tel: (212) 832-1551

Mustard Grille
50 Burnhamthorpe Road West
Mississauga, Ontario L5B-3C2
Canada
Tel: (905) 270-2255

On Canon
301 North Canon Drive
Beverly Hills, California 90210
United States
Tel: (310) 247-2900

Opus 251
251 South 18th Street
Philadelphia, Pennsylvania 19103
United States
Tel: (215) 735-6787
Fax: (215) 735-6170

Pinot Bistro
12969 Ventura Boulevard
Studio City, California 91604
United States
Tel: (818) 990-0500

Provence Restaurant
2401 Pennsylvania Avenue N.W.
Washington, D.C. 20007
United States
Tel: (202) 296-1166

Rain
100 West 82nd Street
New York, New York 10024
United States
Tel: (212) 501-0776

Raku-an Asian Diner
1900 Q Street N.W.
Washington, D.C. 20039
United States
Tel: (202) 265-7258

Regata Cafe
87 Hayarkon Street
Tel Aviv 63432
Israel
Tel: (972) 3-527-8666

Republic
37 Union Square West
New York, New York 10003
United States
Tel: (212) 627-7172
Fax: (212) 627-7010

Rococo
123 Chestnut Street
Philadelphia, Pennsylvania 19106
United States
Tel: (215) 629-1100
Fax: (215) 629-3666

Spezzo Ristorante
140 York Boulevard
Richmond Hill, Ontario L4B-1J8
Canada
Tel: (905) 886-9703

Spiga Ristorante
718 Central Avenue
Scarsdale, New York 10583
United States
Tel: (914) 725-8240
Fax: (914) 725-4668

Stir Crazy Cafe
2171 Northbrook Court
Northbrook, Illinois 60062
United States
Tel: (847) 562-4800
Fax: (847) 562-4805

Tammany Hall
393 Third Avenue
New York, New York 10016
United States
Tel: (212) 696-2001

T.H.A.I. in Shirlington
4029 South 28th Street
Arlington, Virginia 22206
United States
Tel: (703) 931-3203

Tosca
14 North Street
Hingham, Massachusetts 02043
United States
Tel: (617) 740-0080
Fax: (617) 740-0440

Vertigo Restaurant & Bar
Transamerica Pyramid
600 Montgomery Street
San Francisco, California 94111
United States
Tel: (415) 433-7250
Fax: (415) 732-7270

Water Grill
544 South Grand Avenue
Los Angeles, California 90071
United States
Tel: (213) 891-0900
Fax: (213) 629-1891

Zen Palate
611 Ninth Avenue
New York, New York 10036
United States
Tel: (212) 582-1669

Zen Palate
34 East Union Square
New York, New York 10003
United States
Tel: (212) 614-9291

Zen Palate
2170 Broadway
New York, New York 10024
United States
Tel: (212) 501-7761

ARCHITECTS & INTERIOR DESIGNERS

Adam D. Tihany International, Ltd.
57 East 11th Street
New York, New York 10003
United States
Tel: (212) 505-2360
Fax: (212) 529-3578

**Adamstein & Demetriou
Architecture & Design**
2501 M Street N.W.
Washington, D.C. 20037
United States
Tel: (202) 333-9038
Fax: (202) 955-9209

**Arthur de Mattos Casas
Arquitectura Design**
Alameda Ministro Rocha Azevedo, 1052
São Paulo, São Paulo 01410002
Brazil
Tel: (55) 11-282-6311
Fax: (55) 11-282-6608

Bentel & Bentel Architects
22 Buckram Road
Locust Valley, New York 11560
United States
Tel: (516) 676-2880

**Bogdanow Partners
Architects, P.C.**
75 Spring Street
New York, New York 10012
United States
Tel: (212) 966-0313
Fax: (212) 941-8875

Brantner Design Associates
2940 Nebraska Avenue
Santa Monica, California 90404
United States
Tel: (310) 264-5450
Fax: (310) 264-5452

Cricket Design Company, Inc.
235 Carlaw Avenue
Toronto, Ontario M4M-2S1
Canada
Tel: (416) 463-1874
Fax: (416) 466-2244

DiCicco Vinci • Ahn Architects
135 Fifth Avenue
New York, New York 10010
United States
Tel: (212) 673-5495
Fax: (212) 673-5930

Engstrom Design Group
1414 Fourth Street
San Rafael, California 94901
United States
Tel: (415) 454-2277
Fax: (415) 454-2278

Felderman and Nadel (currently Felderman + Keatinge Assoc.)
1800 Berkeley Street
Santa Monica, California 90404
United States
Tel: (310) 452-1445
Fax: (310) 452-6151

Floss Barber, Inc.
Floss Barber
117 South 17th Street
Philadelphia, Pennsylvania 19103
United States
Tel: (215) 557-0700
Fax: (215) 557-6700

Harman Jablin Architects
280 East 45th Street
New York, New York 10017
United States
Tel: (212) 949-6161
Fax: (212) 949-6769

Hatch Design Group
3198-D Airport Loop Drive
Costa Mesa, California 92626
United States
Tel: (714) 979-8385
Fax: (714) 979-6430

Haverson Architecture & Design, P.C.
289 Greenwich Avenue
Greenwich, Connecticut 06830
United States
Tel: (203) 629-8300
Fax: (203) 629-8399

Jordan Mozer & Associates, Ltd.
320 West Ohio Street
Chicago, Illinois 60610
United States
Tel: (312) 397-1133
Fax: (312) 397-1233

Martin Hirschberg Design Associates Ltd.
334 Queen Street East
Toronto, Ontario M5A-1S8
Canada
Tel: (416) 868-1210
Fax: (416) 868-6650

Marve Cooper Design
2120 West Grand Avenue
Chicago, Illinois 60612
United States
Tel: (312) 733-4250
Fax: (312) 733-9715

Morris Nathanson Design
163 Exchange Street
Pawtucket, Rhode Island 02860
United States
Tel: (401) 723-3800
Fax: (401) 723-3813

Studio GAIA
11 Garden Court
Tenafly, New Jersey 07670
United States
Tel/Fax: (201) 541-1887

STUDIOS Architecture
1133 Connecticut Avenue N.W.
Washington, D.C. 20036
United States
Tel: (202) 736-5900
Fax: (202) 736-5959

To Design
424 Marine Street
Point Richmond, California 94801
United States
Tel: (415) 332-8848
Fax: (415) 339-2755

Tony Chi & Associates
215 Park Avenue South
New York, New York 10003
United States
Tel: (212) 353-8860
Fax: (212) 673-1454

Torchia Associates, Inc.
750 North Orleans Street
Chicago, Illinois 60610
United States
Tel: (312) 664-3346
Fax: (312) 664-1599

PHOTOGRAPHERS

Theodore Adamstein
2501 M Street N.W.
Washington, D.C. 20037
United States
Tel: (202) 333-9038
Fax: (202) 955-9209

Dennis E. Anderson
48 Lucky Drive
Greenbrae, California 94904
United States
Tel: (415) 927-3530
Fax: (415) 927-2659

Arch Photo, Inc.
Eduard Hueber
51 White Street
New York, New York 10013
United States
Tel: (212) 941-9294

Robert Vance Blosser
34 East 30th Street
New York, New York 10016
United States
Tel: (212) 679-2802
Fax: (212) 779-9281

Catherine Tighe Bogert
P.O. Box 89
Lambertville, New Jersey 08530
United States
Tel/Fax: (609) 397-8966

David Clifton
2637 West Winnemac Avenue
Chicago, Illinois 60625
United States
Tel: (312) 334-4346
Fax: (312) 275-4175

Tom Crane
113 Cumberland Place
Bryn Mawr, Pennsylvania 19010
United States
Tel: (610) 525-2444
Fax: (610) 527-7529

Nagamitsu Endo
53 3rd Street
Brooklyn, New York 11231
United States
Tel: (718) 643-9758

Esto Photographics
Peter Aaron
222 Valley Place
Mamaroneck, New York 10543
United States
Tel: (914) 698-4060
Fax: (914) 698-1033

Martin Fine
10072 Larwin Avenue
Chatsworth, California 91311
United States
Tel/Fax: (818) 341-7113

Kwoi Gin
474 Bathurst Street
Toronto, Ontario M5T-3S6
Canada
Tel: (416) 924-4883
Fax: (416) 975-4060

Douglas Hill
2324 Moreno Drive
Los Angeles, California 90039
United States
Tel/Fax: (213) 660-0681

Interior Images
Richard Johnson
2 Glengannon Drive
Toronto, Ontario M4B-2W4
Canada
Tel: (416) 755-7742
Fax: (416) 755-9622

Warren Jagger
150 Chestnut Street
Providence, Rhode Island 02904
United States
Tel: (401) 351-7366
Fax: (401) 421-7567

Andrew Kramer
6317 Arapahoe Road
Boulder, Colorado 80303
United States
Tel: (303) 449-2280
Fax: (303) 449-7177

Norman McGrath
164 West 79th Street
New York, New York 10024
United States
Tel: (212) 799-6422
Fax: (212) 799-1285

Milroy & McAleer Photography
Mark Milroy
711 West 17th Street
Costa Mesa, California 92627
United States
Tel: (714) 722-6402
Fax: (714) 722-6371

Peter Paige
269 Parkside Road
Harrington Park, New Jersey 07640
United States
Tel: (201) 767-3150
Fax: (201) 767-9263

Tuca Reinés
Rua Emanuel Kant 58
São Paulo, São Paulo 04536050
Brazil
Tel: (55) 11-306-19127
Fax:: (55) 11-852-8735

Dub Rogers
330 Third Avenue
New York, New York 10010
United States
Tel/Fax: (212) 696-4174

Cesar Rubio
2565 3rd Street
San Francisco, California 94107
United States
Tel: (415) 550-6369
Fax: (415) 285-4784

Steinkamp/Ballogg Photography
Mark Ballogg
666 West Hubbard Street
Chicago, Illinois 60610
United States
Tel: (312) 421-1233
Fax: (312) 421-1241

Tim Street-Porter
2074 Watsonia Terrace
Los Angeles, California 90068
United States
Tel: (213) 874-4278
Fax: (213) 876-8795

Jeffrey Totaro
406 Fitzwater Street
Philadelphia, Pennsylvania 19147
United States
Tel: (215) 925-3732

WALD s.r.l.
Maurizio Mercato
Via Apollo XI
37050 S. Maria DiZevio
Verona
Italy
Tel: (39) 45-605-0601
Fax: (39) 45-605-0146

Paul Warchol
133 Mulberry Street
New York, New York 10013
United States
Tel: (212) 431-3461
Fax: (212) 274-1953

Matt Wargo
4236 Main Steet
Philadelphia, Pennsylvania 19127
United States
Tel:: (215) 483-1211
Fax: (215) 483-9350

Kenneth M. Wyner
7313 Baltimore Avenue
Takoma Park, Maryland 20912
United States
Tel: (301) 495-9475
Fax: (301) 495-9473

Wade Zimmerman
9 East 97th Street
New York, New York 10029
United States
Tel: (212) 427-8784
Fax: (212) 427-3526

INDEX